Crafting with Wood: Your Complete Starter Guide to Woodworking

Billyh Q. Garcia

Introduction

Welcome to the world of woodworking! In this guide, we'll walk you through the exciting world of woodworking projects and plans, perfect for beginners eager to embark on their crafting journey.

Before diving into the projects, let's explore the benefits of woodworking in the "Benefits of Woodworking" section. From the satisfaction of creating something with your own hands to the therapeutic and stress-relieving aspects, you'll discover why woodworking is a rewarding and enjoyable hobby.

To start your woodworking journey, "How to Choose the Right Woodworking Project" offers essential tips on selecting the perfect project that matches your interests, skills, and available tools and materials. From there, "Measuring Tips" and "Essential Tools & Materials" sections provide valuable insights and guidelines for accurate measurements and the necessary tools to have in your woodworking arsenal.

Choosing the right wood is crucial in woodworking, and "Choosing the Right Wood to Use" section helps you navigate the variety of wood types available. Consider factors like suitability for your project, price, and specific wood characteristics. With "Types of Wood" as your guide, you'll gain knowledge about various wood species and their unique features.

Safety is paramount in woodworking, and "Woodworking Safety Tips" section provides a comprehensive list of safety practices to follow during your woodworking adventures. From wearing proper safety equipment to keeping your workspace organized, safety is always a top priority.

Now, it's time to delve into the woodworking projects! In the "Simple DIY Woodworking Projects" section, you'll find a range of beginner-friendly projects to hone your skills. From floating shelves to a rustic hairpin leg wine holder, these projects will spark your creativity and give you a sense of accomplishment.

For those looking to challenge themselves, "Intermediate and Advanced DIY Woodworking Projects" offers more complex projects, like a model airplane and a step stool with dovetail joints. These projects will take your woodworking skills to the next level and showcase your craftsmanship.

Finally, "Tips on Staining and Finishing" provides guidance on how to add the perfect finishing touches to your woodworking creations. With these staining and finishing tips, your projects will have a professional and polished look.

So, whether you're a woodworking novice or have some experience under your belt, this guide will help you embark on a fulfilling and rewarding woodworking journey. Get ready to craft, create, and enjoy the art of woodworking!

Contents

CHAPTER 1

WOOD WORKING 101

Woodworking is a fun activity. Plus, it's a practical skill. You can use it to earn money and perhaps, start your own business.

BENEFITS OF WOODWORKING

Here are just some of the reasons to start woodworking:

It helps you save money.

A piece of furniture can cost you an arm and a leg. So, if you want to save some cash, it's a great idea to make your own furniture. Woodworking saves you $50 to $300 a piece. In fact, most of the woodworking plans that you can find later in this book costs less than $50.

It gives you a strong sense of fulfillment.

Completing your own woodworking project is a great achievement. It gives you a strong a feeling of satisfaction. It gives you bragging rights; you get to tell your friends "I made that".

It is a good past time.

If you need a productive past time, woodworking is a good activity to try. It is surprisingly fun and enjoyable. So, instead of just sitting and watching TV, why not do something productive like making your own stool or study table.

You get to learn a new skill.

Woodworking is a special skill that you can use to build a business or start a furniture-making career. It's like learning a new language or learning how to cook or bake.

It improves your health.

Studies show that woodworking has positive effects to your health. It improves your cognitive function as you need to use logic in creating and implementing woodworking plans. It also helps prevent depression as it gives you a strong sense of achievement.

Woodworking also improves your muscle tone and it improves your overall bone health. It promotes joint flexibility and improve your balance. It also helps you control your weight and improves your cardiovascular function. It helps reduce your blood pressure and it's a great stress management tool.

Woodworking is also a great exercise. It helps you burn calories. Increase your muscle strength and metabolism.

It can be a good source of income.

As you improve your woodworking skills over time, you can start selling your woodwork. This would be a great source of income and you can earn a lot of money from this.

HOW TO CHOOSE THE RIGHT WOODWORKING PROJECT

There are a lot of things that you should consider in choosing the right woodworking projects, including:

Budget

How much are you willing to spend on a woodworking project? If you're on a tight budget, maybe you can make rustic stools and decors first. These woodworking projects are cheaper to complete because you'll only use scrap materials.

Time

For most beginners, woodworking is just a pastime. So, it is important to check how many hours can you spare for your project. If you're making something simple like a floating shelf or a wine rack, you'd only need one to three hours. But, if you're building something complicated like a bed or a desk, you're going to need a day or two to complete the project.

Skill Level

You also need to consider your skill level in choosing the right project for you. It's best to pick simply woodworking projects first like wine holders, stools, and simple study table.

Need

Of course, you have to determine what type of woodworking project do you need. Do you need a new bed or a new chair?

MEASURING TIPS

Woodworking is quite like life. You'd learn best from experience. But, the best measuring tip you'll ever hear is "measure twice and cut once".

Here are some practical measuring tips that you can use:

Pick the right tape measure.

There are a lot of kinds of tape measures, including surveyors tape measures, pocket tape measures, specialist tape measure, keyring tape measure, auto lock tape measure, and many more. When you're doing woodworking, it is best to use a tape measure that has inch marks and feet marks. Make sure that the marks are easy to read. Make sure that there's no additional markings that can cause confusion.

Burn an inch.

Most tape measures has riveted ends, usually by an inch or less. So to get a more accurate measurement, it's good to burn an inch. This means that you have to start measuring on the one inch mark.

Don't bend the measuring tape.

If you're measuring a corner, do not bend it as this will give you an inaccurate measurement. Take separate measurement for the vertical and the horizontal line.

Follow the plans.

For beginners, it's best to follow the woodworking plan strictly. But, over time, you can tweak the plans a little bit and personalize it.

Use a marker or a pencil.

It is necessary to use a marker or a pencil. This will make it easier for you to cut your wood pieces more accurately. Use a ruler to make sure that your line is straight.

Photo Source: htoolwoodworking.com

Lastly, invest in good measuring materials because in woodworking, measurement is everything.

Choosing Your Workspace

You can use your garage or basement as a workspace. But, if you want to turn this into a career, you can later on build your own workshop in your backyard. Your workspace must be safe and it must be enclosed so you will not disturb your family members and friends with all the noise.

Woodworking is fun and exciting, too. Who knows? Maybe, your woodworking skills will be your ticket out of your day job and into the world of business.

CHAPTER 2

ESSENTIAL TOOLS & MATERIALS

To get started, you'll need essential woodworking materials. Here are the basic woodworking materials that you would need:

Jig saw – This woodworking tool will help you cut curves.

Photo Source: Amazon.com

Hand Saws – You need these tools for cross cutting and straightening edges. It also enables you to cut down boards to the final width.

Power drill – You'll need this to drill holes for screws and other connectors.

Photo Source: amazon.com

Circular Saw – You'll need this for rough dimensioning. You'll also need this for long rip cuts.

Chisel – You'll need this to shape a cutting edge.

Claw Hammer – This will help you secure nails into the wood. This probably the most basic woodworking tool that you'll ever need.

Clamps – You'll need clamps if you're planning to make a lot of woodwork project. This will help tighten and secure woodworks such as beds and tables.

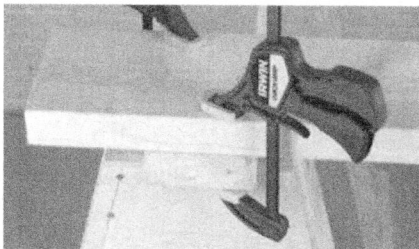

Photo Source: ezwoodshop.com

Tape Measure – This is one of the essential woodworking tools. It's best to use a 25 foot rolling tape measure so it's easier to roll and easier to use.

Utility Knife – You can use this amazing tool to scribe wood and clean out mortise joints.

Level – To ensure that your woodwork is straight, you need to use the level. If you're doing a basic furniture project, you won't need the 6 foot level that construction people use. You'll probably need a 48-inch level.

Screw Driver – You'll need a good set of screwdrivers to get started. Here's a list of screwdrivers that you may need:

- **Phillips** – This is the most common screw driver. It has a cross in the middle of the head. Each cross blade is tapered at 57 degrees. The Phillips screw driver comes in different sizes, the smallest of which is called the "jeweler's screwdriver."

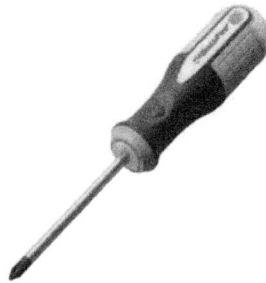

Photo Source: amazon.com

- **Slot Head** – This is the original style of screw driver. It has a slotted line across its head. This screwdriver is less common nowadays, but you can still use it in woodworking.

- **Pozidriv** – This is the enhanced version of the Phillips screw drive. Aside from the cross, it also four recessed radial lines in between each "cross" line. The radial lines create additional contact points.

- **Square Recess** – This has a recessed square. The driver is also shaped like a square. This driver is usually used in furniture-making.

- **Torx** – This is commonly used for electronic and automotive items.

- **Hex** – This has a six sided fastener head, hence the name. This screw drive is usually used in building furnitures.

Nail Set – Woodworking beginners should have a good nail set. Having different nail sizes will save you time.

Sliding T Bevel – You'll need this tool to duplicate an existing angle. You can also use it to set a desired angle. You can use it with other measuring tools such as framing square and protractor.

Smoothing Plane – This will smoothen your wood surface and will help you achieve a more polished look.

Screw Gun – This tool is a bit similar to a power drill, but it is specifically used to drive screws.

Layout Square – This is also known as speed square. It's used for determining and marking angles. It is also used in making square cuts on wood boards.

Caliper - This is a device that's used to measure the distance between the opposite sides of an object. This device is typically used in woodworking, but it is also used in other fields such as engineering, metalworking, science, forestry, and medicine.

Framing Square – This is typically known as the Carpenter's square. This is used to lay out right angles and squares.

Feather Board – This is a safety device that is typically used when working with power saws and stationary routers. It applies pressure on the workpiece keeping it flat against the machine table.

Saw Horse – This is a beam with four legs. This is used to support a plank or board.

Work Bench – This is a sturdy table that is used by woodworkers to hold workpieces.

Tool Storage System – To get started, you'll need a toolbox. It is a box that is used to carry, organize, and protect your woodworking tools. You can get a simple toolbox or you can opt for alternatives such as tool sets, tool chest, tool belts, auto carts, and workshop trolley.

Palm Sander – This is a power tool that you typically use to smooth surfaces. There are many types of sanders that you can use including:

- Detail Sander
- Orbital Sander

- Disc Sander
- Random Orbital Sander
- Wide Belt Sander
- Profile Shaper
- Belt Sander
- Flap Sander

Miter Gauge – This is used to make accurate miters and crosscuts in a wood workpiece.

Band Saw – This is a power tool that is used to cut timbers. It is also used to cut metals.

Photo Source: craftsman.cm

Radial Arm Saw – This is a cutting machine that contains a circular saw that's mounted on a sliding arm. This is an older version of the miter saw so it's much cheaper. If you're on a budget, it may be a great idea to purchase this instead of the miter saw.

Drill Press – This is a fixed-style drill that's mounted on a stand. A drill press is better than hand-held drill because it takes less effort to apply the drill to the wood.

Coping Saw – This is a hand saw that's used to cut intricate internal and external cutouts. It is also used to cut moldings.

Crosscut Saw – This is used to cut wood across the wood grain.

Rip Saw – This is a wood saw that's used to make a rip cut.

Slip Joint Pliers – Slip joint pliers are used to grip something round or cut cords. You can also use it to twist wires.

Diagonal Cutters – Every now and then, you may have to deal with metals and aluminums. Diagonal cutters are used for cutting brass, copper, iron, and steel wire.

Rasp – This tool is used to shape wood and carving surfaces.

Hand Scrapers – This tool is used to scrape metal from a surface. It is also used to scrape wood.

Doweling Jigs – This helps you drill a straight hole in a precise location. This is helpful when you are doweling two or more workpieces together.

Router – This is a tool that you use to route out an area. This is usually used in building cabinets.

Drill – This is a tool that's used for boring holes in wood pieces and metal. It is also used to fasten wood pieces together.

Spade Shaped Drill Bits – This is used to create different kind of holes. This is very useful in connecting different types of wood together.

You'd also need screws, paint, paint brushes, varnish and many more. But, stick to these basics first. You may need to upgrade your tools later on.

Your tools will determine the quality of your work. So, if you want to turn woodworking into a career or business, you have to invest in good materials.

CHAPTER 3

CHOOSING THE RIGHT WOOD TO USE

To ensure that your work is durable and of high quality, you have to choose the right type of wood. Here are some of the tips that can help you choose the right wood for your project:

THINK ABOUT WHAT'S SUITABLE FOR WHAT YOU'RE BUILDING.

Should you use hard wood or soft wood? Well, the answer is it depends on what you're building. If you're building a sophisticated dining table or a queen bed, then hardwood would be a good choice. But, if you're building a workbench or a simple study table, you can go for pine plywood.

Softwoods are evergreen trees while hardwoods come from flowering trees. Although some softwoods are actually hard, hardwoods are generally more stable and stronger so it's perfect for construction. Softwoods, on the other hand, are perfect for carvings.

Here are the common hardwoods:

Red ash

White ash

Beech

Yellow birch

Balsa

European ash

Cherry

Butternut

Kingwood

Rosewood

Sycamore

Purpleheart

Teak

Tulipwood

Lime

Mahogany

Walnut

Ebony

Maple

Kingwood

Oak

Here's a list of the common softwoods:

Cedar

Fir

Larch

Pine

Redwood

Yew

If durability is your priority, it's best to use Chestnut, Iroko, Spanish Cedar, or Oak wood.

CONSIDER THE PRICE.

If you're on a budget, it would a good idea to go for pine wood. Pine wood cracks but it is cheap and easy to find. Try to avoid using extremely expensive wood such as sandalwood, ebony, purple heart, and Dalbergia, but as much as you can, go for the best you can afford.

CHECK FOR THE FOLLOWING CHARACTERISTICS:

To build a high quality project, you need to choose nothing but the best wood. In choosing the right wood for your woodworking project, you need to look for the following characteristics:

Hardness – Remember that not all hardwoods are hard and not all softwoods are soft. So, it's important to actually test the hardness of the wood and not just rely on its botanical classification. But, in general, hardwoods are more durable and valuable than softwood.

Grade – Not all woods are equal, so you need to look at the grade of the wood. If you want to build a high quality furniture, it's best to use FAS, FAS 1-FACE, Sound Wormy, Selects, and No. 1 Common.

CONSIDER YOUR SKILL LEVEL.

For woodworking beginners, it's best to use fir and pine. These are not as high quality as maple or mahogany, but they are easier to work with. So, you can use pine first and then use higher quality wood later, after you have mastered the woodworking craft.

TYPES OF WOOD

Here's a list of the best woods that you can use for woodworking:

Oak

This is the most used hardwoods. It is heavy and it has a light color. It is used typically for English and American woodworking designs.

Photo Source: wood-database.com

Maple

There are about 115 species of maple. Some are hard and some are soft. Hard maple is too hard that it's really difficult to work with. So, if you're a beginner, it's best to work with soft maple.

Cedar

This is a reddish wood that is relatively soft. It has a straight grain and it smells really good. This is best for outdoor furniture projects such as patio tables because it can handle moist areas.

Fir

This wood has a pronounced, straight, and reddish brown tint. It is often used for building, but since it's relatively cheap, it is commonly used for furniture-making, too.

Pine

Photo Source: realsimple.com

This is the perfect choice for beginners because it is cheap and easy to work with. It is also perfect for carving. But, you should avoid using this if you're making a sophisticated piece of furniture such as a wooden sofa, dining table, or an intricate bed.

Redwood

This is typically used for outdoor furniture because of its amazing resistance to moisture. It has a straight grain and it has a reddish color. It's not cheap, but it's not expensive either.

Ash

Ash has a straight grain and like the pine, it is very easy to work with.

Birch

There are two types of birch trees – while and yellow. This wood is readily available and it is definitely cheaper than many hardwoods. It is stable and it is also easy to work with.

Cherry

It's easy to find cherry wood. It has a reddish brown color and it is commonly used for woodworking and furniture-making. This wood is easy to work with but it is relatively more expensive than maple or oak.

Mahogany

This is one of the most amazing furniture woods. It has a reddish brown color and it is incredibly durable. It takes stain well, so you'll only need to apply one coat of varnish to give it a polished look.

Poplar

This is one of the less expensive hardwoods. It is soft and very easy to work with. It is a good choice of drawers. It is stable.

Teak

This is a rare type of hardwood, but this is perfect for outdoor furniture. It is weather-resistant and it is beautiful, too. It has a golden-brown color and an oily feel.

Walnut

This is really easy to work with and this is perfect for big projects like queen-size beds or dining tables. This is also quite expensive.

Remember that in woodworking, the quality of the wood is everything. But, if you're a beginner, it's best to pick the woods that are easier to work with. Then, as you progress, you may use harder and more expensive wood.

CHAPTER 4

WOODWORKING SAFETY TIPS

Woodworking is fun, but it can be dangerous, too. Remember that you'll be dealing with power tools and heavy wood pieces. Accidents can happen so you need to observe the following safety tips:

ALWAYS WEAR SAFETY EQUIPMENT.

This is the most important safety rule that you should observe. You'll need to use:

- Safety glasses – This will protect your eyes.
- Hearing protection – This will protect your ears.
- Face masks – Sanding wood can create a lot of dust so you need to protect your face.
- Face shield – A full face shield will protect you from flying chips.

WEAR PROPER CLOTHING.

It is important to wear comfortable clothing. This will make it easier for you to move and carry things.

DISCONNECT THE POWER BEFORE BLADE CHANGES.

Power saws are dangerous, so it is important to disconnect the power before you change blades.

DO NOT USE MULTIPLE EXTENSION CORDS.

To prevent fire or electrical problems, it's best to only use one extension cord.

USE SHARP BLADES.

Dull cutting tools are dangerous, so make sure to sharpen your blades regularly.

ORGANIZE YOUR NAILS WELL.

Do not leave nails lying around the floor. Make sure that your nails are well organized all the time.

FOCUS

To prevent accidents, you have to avoid distractions and focus on the task at hand.

Your safety should be your top priority.

CHAPTER 5

SIMPLE DIY WOODWORKING PROJECTS

Here are some practical and easy to follow plans that you can use to build basic furniture like a stool or shelves.

DIY FLOATING SHELVES

Shelves are relatively easy to do and they are extremely useful, too. So, to get started, here are some amazing DIY shelf projects that you can do:

This is an easy and useful woodworking project that you can complete in an hour or two.

To do this, you'll need:

- Clamps
- Drill or screwdriver
- Screws
- 2 pieces of ¼ inches x 2 feet x 4 ft sanded plywood panel
- 2 pieces of 1 inch x 2 inches x 8 feet select pine board
- Stud finder
- Level
- Paint brush
- Painter's tape with Edge
- Paint or varnish

Directions:

Step 1

Cut the wood pieces below into the following dimensions. To have the precise size you can just ask assistance from the staff of any depot store or hardware store you will visit for these materials.

- 4 – 1-in. x 2-in. x 21-in.
- 8 – 1-in. x 2-in. x 6½ in.
- 4 – ¼-in. x 8-in. x 21-in.
- 4 – ¼-in. x 2-in. x 8-in.
- 2 – ¼-in. x 2-in. x 21⅜-in.

Step 2

Screw these wood pieces together to make your frame. Your frame should look like this:

Photo Source: younghouselove.com

Step 3

Glue, nail, or clamp the sanded panels to the frame. Attach the shelf to the using using a screw driver. Then, screw at least one stud finder for stability.

Step 4

Once you're certain that the shelf is leveled, add the remaining screws. Then, attach the second floating shelf. Make sure that it has the same measurements.

Step 5

Attach the 1 inch by 2-inch boards to the front of both shelves. Glue the remaining ¼ inch boards to the front. Once the glue is dry, paint the shelves.

Photo Source: pinterest

This project is fun and it is really easy to do. You can place these shelves in your bathroom, bedroom, or living room.

DIY HONEYCOMB SHELVES

Honeycomb shelves are easy on the eyes and you can place just about anything on them – books, figurines, scented candles, and porcelain decors.

To make your own honeycomb shelves, you'll need:

- Miter saw
- Wood screws
- Drill
- Drill bit
- Level
- Rotary sander
- Tape measure
- Wall brackets
- Wood glue
- 3 Fencing planks
- Marker

Directions:

Step 1

Set your miter saw to cut your planks at 30 degree angle. After you make the first cut, turn the plank over and measure the long ledge. Make sure that the long ledge is 12 inches. Mark the spot where you want to make your next cut. Then, make the second cut. You now have the first piece for your honeycomb shelves.

Step 2

Repeat the process. You'll need to cut fifteen 12-inch pieces. Make sure that all 15 pieces have the exact same size.

Step 3

To make one hexagon pod, you have to take 6 pieces of wood and set them standing on the floor. Connect these pieces to form a hexagon. You'll feel like you're connecting a puzzle. Use a wood club to connect the pieces together. Press the sides tightly.

Step 4

Using a drill bit and a drill, pre-drill the holes when you want to screw and connect two hexagons together. This will make it easier for you to screw and it prevents the wood from cracking, too.

Step 5

Repeat steps 3 and 4 until you're done with your first hexagon. Then, repeat the process until you've made three connected hexagons. Your honeycomb shelf should look like this:

Step 6

Photos: friedasophie.blogspot.com

To hang your shelf, find the studs and then screw your brackets into them. Screw the bottom part of the bracket first and then put some pressure to the top bracket. Make sure that it is durable and it can hold some weight.

Step 7

Rest your shelf on the bracket. Then, go ahead and mark where you'll put your next bracket. Put as many brackets as necessary for reinforcement. Now, you're done!

This honeycomb shelf is fun, attractive, and surprisingly easy to make. This is a project that you can do with your friends and even your kids.

LEATHER STRAP SHELF

Photo Source: cleverlittlemonkey.com

This is an awesome and chic shelf that will add a lot of personality to any room.

Materials:

- Screw gun
- Staple gun
- 1 inch wide leather strap
- 1x6 inch plywood
- Paint (Any color will do)

Directions:

Step 1

Paint the plywood and let it dry for a few minutes.

Step 2

Bring the ends of the 1 inch leather strap together. Fold the ends over twice. Then, fold the ends of the strap to the wall using a screw gun.

Step 3

Slip the painted plywood into the leather loop. The leather strap should be at least three inches from the shelf end. Ask someone to hold the second leather strap and then slide the other end of the painted plywood into the second ribbon loop.

Step 4

Use a level to ensure that the shelf is straight. Then affix the second leather strap into the wall using a screw gun. Secure the leather straps under the plywood using a staple gun.

Photo Source: thinkcrafts.com

Remember that this shelf can only hold light objects so try not to put heavy and breakable objects on it.

WOODWORK PLAN FOR A BASIC BOOKSHELF

This woodwork plan is perfect for beginners. You do not need a lot of tools to get this done. This project is incredibly easy to do, this could even be your first wood work project.

Photo Source: thisoldhouse.com

Materials:

- Router
- Electric drill
- Power sander
- Cut off saw
- 2 pieces of 1 x 12 and ¾ of an inch thick pine wood
- 4 pieces of 1 x 11 and ¾ of an inch think pine wood
- 1 piece of 1 x 4 wood
- Table saw
- Clamps
- Carpenter's square
- Deck screw
- 4d finish nails
- Tape measure
- Wood glue

- Screw gun
- Screws
- ¾" nail for the back

Directions:

Step 1

Sand the wood pieces to improve the texture.

Step 2

The longer pieces (1 x 12) will be the upright. So you need to cut a little dado or a slot. It has to be ¾ wide and ¼ inch deep. This will give a place for the shorter shelf boards.to go up into the wood and be securely connected to the longer wood.

Step 3

Cut the two dadoes across the boards using a router. You can also do this with a table saw if you don't have a router.

Step 4

Sand again the dadoes using a power sander. After the wood is sanded, assemble the shelves using a wood glue. Place the glue on the bottom of the dadoes to give an added strength. Then place the boards into the dado slots. Start on one edge and then wiggle it around. Use a hammer to secure the shelf into the dado slots. Clamp it in tight to let the glue set. Clamp it overnight.

Step 5

Take out the clamp. You may need to put a little reinforcement so put in screws in on the side using a screw gun.

Step 6

Put the back onto the shelf. Cut it according to the length and width of your shelf and then nail it to your shelf. If you want, you can paint your shelf.

SIMPLE WORKBENCH

Photo Source: woodgears.ca

If you're serious about woodworking, then you should have a sturdy work bench. Here's a work bench that you can build in less than a day. You need simple tools for this.

Materials

- 2x2s for the frame and legs
- 2 x4 lumber for the frame
- 1/4" plywood that would serve as a workbench top
- Circular saw
- Bar clamps
- Chisel
- Square
- Hand drill
- Screws
- Wood glue

Step 1

Cut the legs. The length has to be 78 centimeters long. Use a measuring tape and a pencil to mark the wood.

Step 2

Now, you need to cut the pieces that connect the legs. Cut four 2 x 4 pieces that's about 55 centimeters long. Then, assemble the frame by screwing and nailing the pieces together.

Step 3

Then, drill on each edge of the frame and attach the legs. Then, place the screws in the pre-drilled holes.

Step 4

Then, screw the rails to the legs. It's easier to do this if the bench is lying on its side.

Step 5

Photo Source: woodgears.ca

Cut the plywood to fit the size of the frame. Then, screw the top of the workbench from the below.

Now you're done! This workbench only cost around $15! Think of all the money that you'll be saving when you make your own furniture.

THREE LEGGED STOOL

Photo Source: etsy.com

Materials

- Pine log
- Screws
- Power Sander or Sand Paper
- Varnish
- Band saw
- Planer
- Three aspen logs
- Knife
- 3 aspen logs
- Hammer
- Nails

Directions

Step 1

Cut a piece of wood from the log using a chainsaw

Step 2

Trim the wood into about two inches thick.

Step 3

Mark a circle on the wood and cut the circle using a band saw

Step 4

Then, flatten the surface using a planer. Then cut three 14 inch aspen logs. This will serve as the legs of your stool.

Step 5

Peel the aspen logs using a knife. Then, sand them.

Step 6

Nail the legs to pine log using a hammer. Then, paint the stool with varnish. Let it dry.

Now, you have a stool! You can make as many stools as you like.

SIMPLE CHAIR

Photo Source: annawhite.com

This is a simple 2 x 4 chair plan that you can implement in just a few hours.

Dimensions

17 ½" x 18 1/2" x 37 ¼"

Materials

- 2 pieces of 10 feet long 2x4s
- 1 piece of 8 feet long 2x4
- Drill
- Saw
- 2 ½" screws
- 4" screws
- Wood filler
- Wood glue
- Paint

- Sander

Cut List

A – 2 pieces of 37 ¾ for back legs

B – 4 pieces of 10 ½" for back and front boards

C – 2 pieces of 16 1/2" for the front legs

D- 2 pieces of 15" side boards

E - 1 piece 13 ½"

F – 3 pieces of 18 ½" for the seat

G – 2 pieces of 17" for the seat side

Directions

Step 1: Build the back.

The first step is to build the back of the chair. You would need to grab the 2 back legs and three front and back boards. Then assemble them following the illustration below. Connect the front and back boards to the legs using 2 ½ pocket screws and Kreg jig. You can also use wood glue.

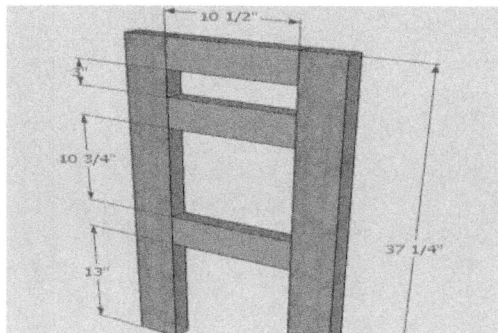

Photo Source: morelikehome.net

Step 2: Assemble the front.

After you build the back, you need to assemble the front using the front legs and the back piece as shown in the picture below:

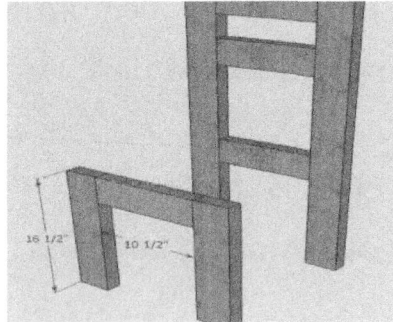

Photo Source: morelikehome.net

Step 3: Assemble the chair.

Use the side board pieces to connect the front and back sections. Screw these pieces into the front and back parts of the chair using a screw gun. Use the illustration below as a guide:

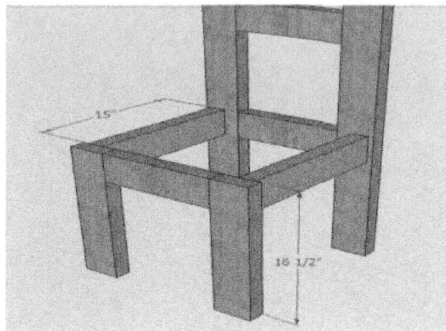

Step 4: Add the support.

Install a 13 1/2 " long at the back of the seat opening. This will give the seat boards an extra space to sit on.

Step 5: Install the seat.

Attach the seat boards using wood glue and screws. Follow the illustrations below.

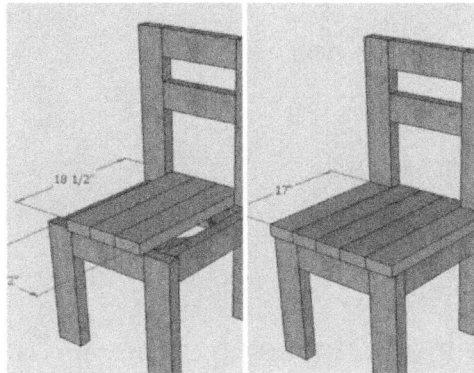

Step 6: Finish up.

Sand the chair and then apply some paint.

PORCH X TABLE

This is a table that's easy to do. You can also place this on your porch or in your kitchen. You can also use this as your kid's study table.

Materials:

- 3 pieces of 20 inch fence posts for the tabletop
- 4 pieces of 1 ½ feet posts
- 4 pieces of wood for the frame
- Screw gun or drill
- Screws

Directions:

Step 1

Assemble the frame using a screw. Then, screw the table top pieces to the frame. It should look like this.

Photo Source: sarahdorseydesigns.com

Step 2

Lay the leg posts in an X position and then connect the two posts together by screwing the middle. Then, attach each X leg on inner edge of your table top.

Photo Source: sarahmdorseydesigns.blogspot.com

Voila, you're done!

A FRAME WINE RACK

Wine racks are easy to do. So, it's best to try this project first before you make something big like a table or a bed.

Photo Source: worldmarket.com

This is a six bottle holder that's very easy to do. To do this, you'll need:

- ✓ 2 pieces of 1" hinges
- ✓ 2 pieces of 15" x 10.5" birch plywood
- ✓ Neon string that's about 12 inches
- ✓ Screwdriver
- ✓ Sand paper
- ✓ Drill with a 1/6" drill bit and 3 ½ " hole saw drill bit
- ✓ Carpenter's square

Directions:

Step 1

Measure and mark where the center of each wine bottle cut-out will go using a carpenter's square and pencil. Each wine bottle should be one inch apart from each other. It should look like this:

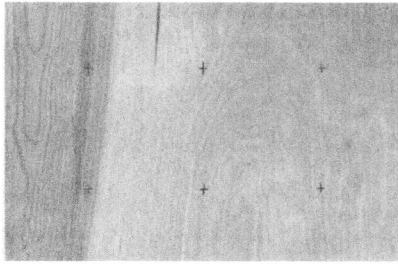

Step 2

Cut out six holes on each plywood so you have a total of twelve holes.

Step 3

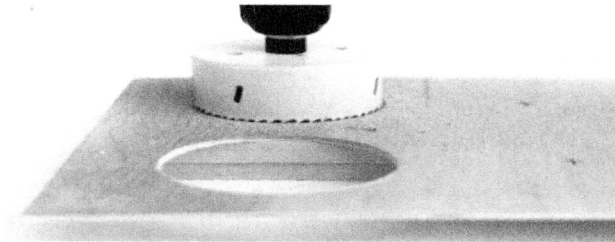

Sand the plywood and then place the hinges on top of the rack. Install one side of the hinge and then repeat on the other side.

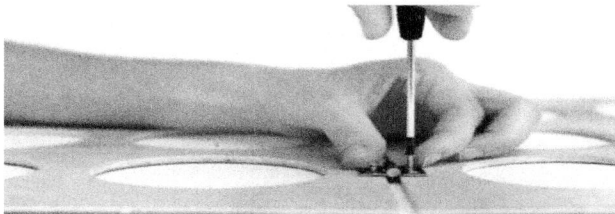

Step 4

Measure one inch from the bottom and side of each plywood and drill a hole on all the four corners of the rack.

Photo Source: diynetwork.com

Step 5

Then, loop the string through one of the holes and then tie to secure. Then loop the string through the opposite hole. Tie a knot and then trim the string. Repeat this process on the other side.

RUSTIC HAIRPIN LEG WINE HOLDER

This piece is perfect if you have a restaurant because it has a strong visual appeal. But, you can place this in your home, too.

Materials:

- ✓ Old crate
- ✓ Hole saw
- ✓ Screw gun
- ✓ Screws
- ✓ 2 Leg pins
- ✓ Pencil or marker
- ✓ Carpenter's square
- ✓ Plywood, about the same size as the crate
- ✓ Plywood

Directions:

Step 1

Using a carpenter square or a ruler, make x mark on the center of where each bottle cut out should go. Then drill 8 holes at the bottom of the crate.

Step 2

Screw the plywood to cover the open part of the crate.

Step 3

Then screw the two hairpin legs on one side of the crate.

Photo Source: momstatic.com

You're done, it's that easy!

CRATE SHOE DISPLAY

If you're a shoe person, you'll definitely want to display your prized possessions. The best way to do this is to create a crate shoe display.

Materials
- ✓ Nails
- ✓ Hammer
- ✓ Sandpaper
- ✓ 6 crates

Directions:

Step 1

Your crate shoe display should look like this:

Photo Source: homejelly.com

So, line up three crates and then nail them together from the side.

Step 2

Then line up another three crates and nail them together to create another rack.

Step 3

Then, nail the two racks together. Sand your shoe rack and you can a paint it if you want.

This shoe rack costs about $5 to $10.

Let the paint dry and then hang the sign in your living room.

This woodworking project will improve your creativity. You can use any color you want. You can also write any funny or inspiring message.

CHAPTER 6

INTERMEDIATE AND ADVANCED DIY WOODWORKING PROJECTS

Here you will find woodworking projects that are a bit more complex than the ones already provided in the previous chapter. These projects require more time and you may need some more experience before trying any of them.

MODEL AIRPLANE

This model airplane is modeled after the World War I fighter planes, although not the exact replica – you'll need really advanced wooworking skills to make exact replicas of those planes.

Materials

- ✓   1 Knot free board (dimensions 1" x 7-1/2" x 24")
- ✓   2 Dowels (7/16" x 1-5/8" / diameter x length)
- ✓   1 Dowel (1/8" x 1" / diameter x length)
- ✓   1 Dowel (1/4" x 24" / diameter x length)

✓   8 Fluted dowels (1/4"x 1" / diameter x length)

Directions:

Step 1

Familiarize yourself with the different parts that you will cut later on. Each part is designated by a letter, such as the following:

A – body

B – engine

C – wing

D – elevator

E – shock absorbers

F – wheel posts

G – shock absorber pins

H – wheels

I – wheel axles

J – propeller

K – nose cone

L – sruts

M – mufflers

N – skid

See the following diagram:

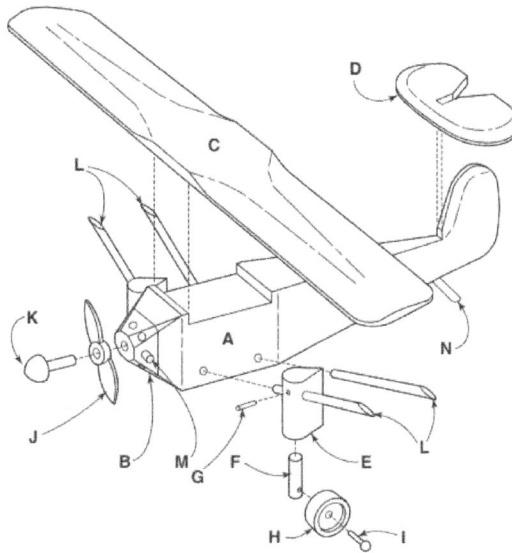

Step 2

Glue together a pair of 1" x 3-1/2" x 11" blocks to make the body. Set it aside to let the glue dry. Now, cut the pieces for the wing, which is a 1/4" x 2-5/8" x 19" block. Make sure to plane the wing piece (marked as C on the diagram above).

Do the same for the blocks for the propeller (1/4" x 1" x 4") and the elevator (1/4" x 2-1/8" x 4-1/4"). Do not cut exactly according to these dimensions. You obviously have more material to work with than you will actually need. When you cut them away, make sure to add a centimeter or so. This will allow you to shave, plane, and sand finish the pieces.

The block for the body should be dry by now. Machine that block to its desired dimensions of 1-7/8" x 3-1/4" x 11". See the following diagram for the dimensions of the said block:

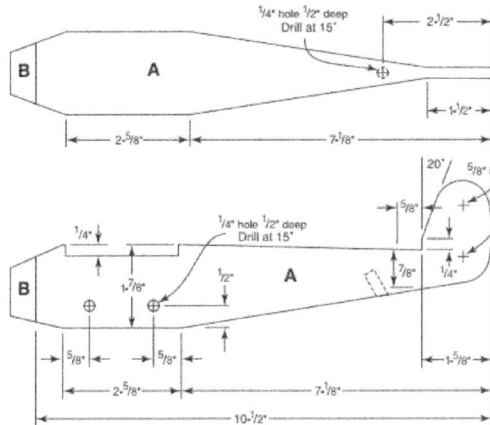

Make sure to mark the locations for the skid and the strut. You should trace the outlines of both the top and side of the body first and then cut them away with a band saw. It will be easier to cut the side profile of the plane first and then you should work on the top and bottom. Cutting the side profile gives you a good idea how to shape the top and bottom later on.

Now you need to make a notch on top of the body for the wing – sketch the area where the notch for the wing will go. The notch should be flat and it should have the following dimensions: 1/4" x 2-5/8" (depth x width). To do that, turn the plane's body on its sides and make quarter inch deep cuts using a band saw– make a cut every 1/8" inches along the notch. Now, chisel away on the material to make the notch flat.

Now you need to make a hole where you can mount the engine piece. It should be about a quarter of an inch deep at the center of the body's front end. It's marked as B in the body diagram above.

Next step, you need to make the engine block. It is shaped like a hexagon and it has the following dimensions: 3/4" x 1-1/2". Remember to give some allowance when you cut to allow you room for sanding and planing.

Drill holes on the engine block for the mufflers (designated in the first diagram as M). These are 1/4" size holes at the center of each side of the octagon on your engine (please see plane illustration for guidance). Drill another ¼" hole this time at the center of the octagon shape of the engine for the propeller. Make sure to drill through.

Now you can glue the engine (block B) to the front of the body (block A). Run a ¼" dowel through the center hole you made to keep the pieces aligned. Set aside and allow the glue to get dried up.

Drill holes for both the skid (marked as N in the plane diagram) and the struts (marked as L in the diagram). Once those holes have been drilled on, file and sand your work. Remove any sharp corners or any saw marks that are visible. File off any part to make it flush with the rest of the airplane's body.

Next, glue the mufflers (marked and designated as M in the airplane diagram). Run them through the engine hub. Leave it it dry for a few minutes. When they are dry, trim the dowels down to ¼"

Step 3

Now it's time to work on the elevator and the airplane's wing. Trace the outline of the wing onto the wooden block, as follows:

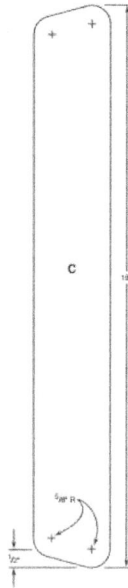

When making the wing, make sure to saw along the grain of the wood. Make sure that the width of the wing will fit flush on the notch you made earlier on the top of the airplane's body.

Center the wing on the airplane's body. You can mark where the wing should meet the notch so that you can be sure that you will position it evenly later. Using a plane, sand paper, file, and spokeshave, shape the airplane's wing.

Next, trace the elevator (marked as D in the diagram). Cut its length giving some material as allowance. File and sand the elevator to its intended shape. See the details below:

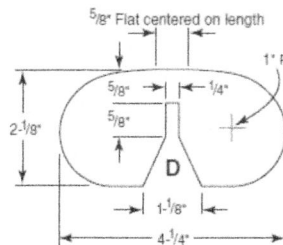

Step 4

Next, make the shock absorbers, wheels, and wheel posts. You will need to cut two shock absorbers and each will have the following dimensions: 3/4" x 4" x 4". The shock absorbers are marked as part E on the complete airplane diagram. You also need to drill a 1/8" hole for the shock absorber pin holes and a ¼" hole for the struts. Please see diagram details below:

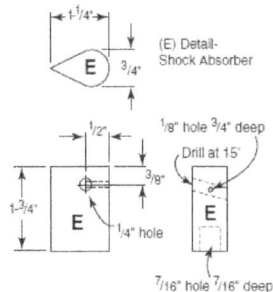

Please refer to full airplane diagram earlier to help you see how each piece should look like. Note that at this point when you work on this plane, it will be a lot easier to work with the larger pieces than with the smaller ones.

Using a file, round over the corners of the airplane's shock absorber blanks. The shock absorbers will have a tear drop like shape. Use a band saw when cutting it. Don't forget to sand away the saw marks on the wood.

After that, you should cut the shock absorbers to 1 ¾" length – its finishing length. Now you can drill the hole for the wheel post (marked F on the airplane diagram).

Use the dowell with the 7/16" diameter to make the wheel posts. Glue these posts to the shock absorbers. Leave it to dry for about a few minutes or until it is completely dried. When the glue has dried, drill a hole that is 7/32" through the airplane's wheel post – you'll mess things up if the glue is still wet.

This hole will be where the wheel axle will go (part marked I on the airplane diagram). Drill a hole this time on the wheel as a counterbore. Make it 1/8" deep. Note that the wheel is marked as H on the airplane diagram. Next, cut the wheels out using a 1 3/8" hole saw. Again, make sure to sand the corners and the saw marks.

Note that there are ready made wheel axles and ready made wheels from various woodworking project centers. You can use them in case you find it difficult to cut and craft the said parts.

Once you have these parts ready you can now insert the wheel axles into the wheels. After that you can then glue the axles to the airplane's wheel posts. Note that you should not glue the wheels on the axles – they should be able to spin freely.

Step 5

Now it's time to make the nose cone as well as the propeller. Trace and cut the following to make the propeller:

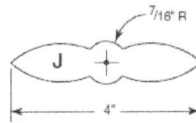

To make the nose cone, you will need to cut away a disc with a 1 inch diameter. The nose cone is marked as part K in the diagram. At the center of the nose cone, drill a quarter in hole that is ¼" inch in depth. Now glue a ¼" dowell into that hole and allow it to dry.

Secure this assembly on a drill chuck and then you should file and sand it into shape. Make sure that the center of the propeller and the nose cone's diameter should match.

Next, work on the skid and the struts. Set the struts in the body of the airplane. Mark a line on the dowell and it should be 4 ¾" from the body of the airplane to the inside edge of the dowell. Cut and sand this part to fit the bottom of the wings.

The skid is marked as part N in the diagram. Glue it to the underside of the airplane – please refer to the diagram.

Glue the wing to the notch you made earlier. Glue the elevator to the tail. Run the nose cone through the propeller and then glue that to the body. Note that the propeller blades should spin freely. Leave the entire assembly to dry for a few minutes.

When it's dry, glue the rear struts to the body and wing. Let them dry. Insert the front struts to the shock absorbers and then glue the struts to the wings and the body of the airplane. Leave it to dry.

Position each shock absorber about half an inch from the body of the airplane. Make sure each shock absorber will remain perpendicular to the plane's wings. Drill a 1/8" hole throught the strut.

Insert the mounting pin for the shock absorber (part marked as G on the diagram). Glue it in place. Allow it to dry. Once dry you can sand it. Finally, you can stain and finish the entire piece according to your liking.

STEP STOOL WITH DOVETAIL JOINTS

This next project makes use of dovetail joints. These types of joints give your pieces that added strength especially when you are using wide boards. If you are able to fit thing snugly, that alone is enough to provide mechanical strength and the needed stability to the stool you're about to craft.

This project will also give you a chance to practice using jigs and routers. You'll be making a through dovetail, straight sliding doevetails, and tapered dovetails.

Tools

- ✓ Clamps
- ✓ Framing square
- ✓ Hammer
- ✓ Half round file
- ✓ Hand plane
- ✓ Dovetail jig
- ✓ Drill
- ✓ Sander
- ✓ Router table
- ✓ ¼" dovetail bit
- ✓ ½" flush cutting bit
- ✓ Router
- ✓ Bandsaw or jigsaw
- ✓ Table saw

Materials

- ✓ 1 piece rails and stretcher – dimensions: 1" x 2" x 12"
- ✓ 1 piece boards for seat, back, and stool front – dimensions: 1" x 10" x 64"
- ✓ 1 piece quarter inch tempered hardboard (template) – 10" x 43"
- ✓ 1 piece half inch plywood base – 10" x 43"
- ✓ 1 piece 1/8" hardboard as spacer – – 10" x 43"
- ✓ 2 pieces ¼" plywood – guideboard for straight socket jig 8 x 12 inches
- ✓ 1 piece plywood – front rail for straight socket jig 2 x 22 inches

✓ 1 piece 1 x 2 scrap wood – back rail for straight socket jig (22")

✓ 2 pieces ¼" plywood – guide board for tapering socket jig (8" x 11-1/2")

✓ 2 pieces 1 x 2 scrap wood – to be used as reference rails for tapering socket jig (21" in length).

Note that the material for the front, seat, and back should come from the same board so that they will have the same grain. For successful dovetails, you should always use flat boards.

Please take the time to review the following diagram:

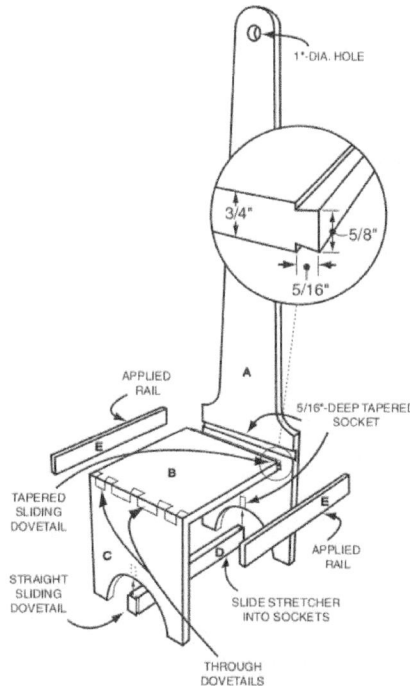

1"-DIA. HOLE

3/4"

5/8"

5/16"

APPLIED RAIL

A

5/16"-DEEP TAPERED SOCKET

E

B

TAPERED SLIDING DOVETAIL

E

APPLIED RAIL

C

D

STRAIGHT SLIDING DOVETAIL

SLIDE STRETCHER INTO SOCKETS

THROUGH DOVETAILS

Here are the dimensions (Thickness x Width x Length) of the parts that you need to precut for this project:

✓ Back part (A) – 3/4" x 9-1/2" x 42-1/4"

✓ Seat part (B) – 3/4" x 9-½" x 11"

✓ Front part (C) – 3/4" x 9-1/2" x 10"

✓ Stretcher part (D) – 3/4" x 1-3/4" x 10-1/2"
✓ Rails (2 pieces) (E) – 5/16" x 1-3/4" x 11-1/2"

Directions:

Step 1

Review the stool diagram. Cut away the seat, front, and back parts of the stool. Make sure that they maintain the same thickness. Allow for some material at the edges for the dovetails that you will make later on.

Step 2

Layout the pattern for the back template on the tempered hardboard as follows:

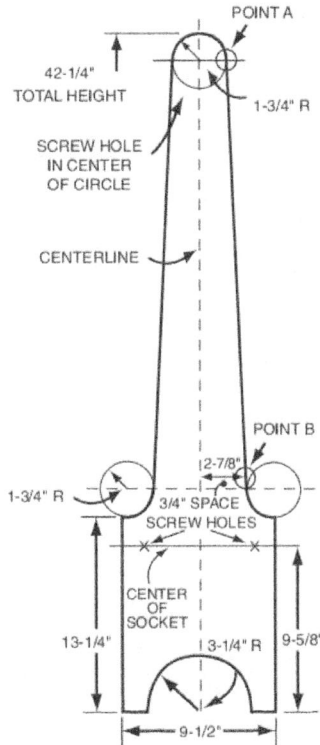

Use a bandsaw or a jigsaw to cut the aforementioned outline. You should cross cut the bottom so that it ends up squared with the sides. Draw that center line that runs across the length of the entire piece.

Draw the circles and arches. Layout the bottom, sides, and top. Cut the edges to the indicated shape. It is now time to cut the sides of this piece into its proper shape.

Using a half round file, smooth the cut curves. Get the side straight with a block plane. Run your hand around the surface to feel for any uneven sides. Sand away to get things even. You usually only need some light sanding at this point.

Step 3

Now it is time to assemble the following three part sandwich setup along with the template:

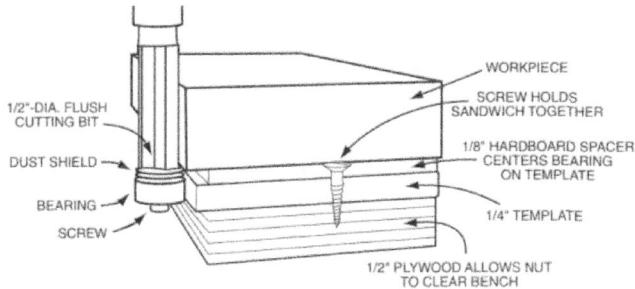

WORKPIECE

SCREW HOLDS
SANDWICH TOGETHER

1/2"-DIA. FLUSH
CUTTING BIT

1/8" HARDBOARD SPACER
CENTERS BEARING
ON TEMPLATE

DUST SHIELD

BEARING

1/4" TEMPLATE

SCREW

1/2" PLYWOOD ALLOWS NUT
TO CLEAR BENCH

Note that template is located at the middle layer.

Step 4

Shape the back and the front parts. Rip the part for the back (part A on the diagram). To rip means to saw along the wood piece's grain. Do the same for the front (pat C on the stool diagram) and the seat (part B). Note that they should be of the same width. Do a cross cut on the front and back parts a little longer than their indicated lengths.

Align the template to the back and trace around the piece. Saw around the traced line but allow about 1/16" from the line that you traced. Next, fasten the template so that it faces side of the back part. After that you should clamp everything to the workbench.

Rout the back counterclockwise. Note that you should rout the curves in one pass with no breaks. Rout the arch of the front board as well. Drill a finger hole at the back that is about an inch in diameter.

The back part and the seat is joined by a sliding dovetail (please see stool diagram). Use a 1/32" thick shim. Taper the guide boards on the table saw for your socket jig. Make sure to size them so that they fit the router base. Rip two pieces of quarter inch plywood according to width.

Tape the shim to the corner edge. Place this edge along the saw fence and then rip again. Cut the other piece in similar fashion. Mark one guide board as X and other as Y.

Make 2 reference rails and nail guideboard X to these rails. Please see the following diagram:

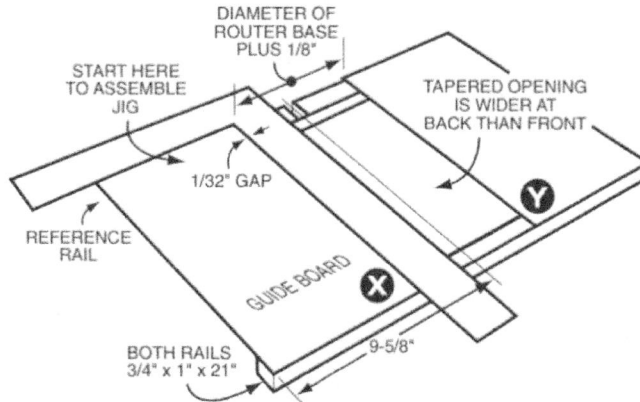

Next, work on the tapered socket using a shank dovetail bit (use a ¼" bit). Set it to a 14 degree pitch. See the following setup:

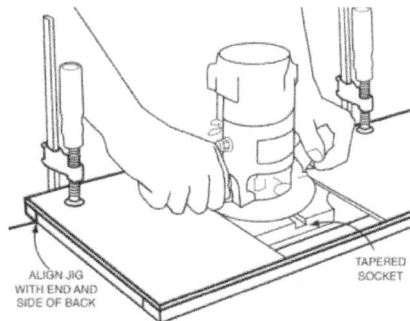

Next, you need to work on the tapered tail for the dovetail on the seat. Use a 1/32" shim on both sides of the seats. Note that you need to adjust the router bit's height so that it is the same depth as the socket. See the following setup:

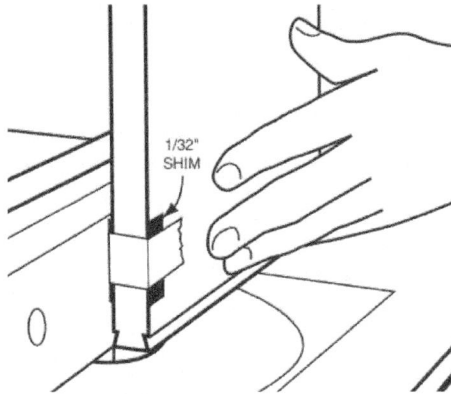

Now you should slide the seat in place and then make sure that it is square with the back part. To get the right length of the front board, you should measure from the bottom of the back part all the way to the top of the seat. Cut the front board according to your measurements.

Step 5

Cut the stretcher sockets. Do it on the inside faces of both the back and the front parts. Fit your router with a straight sided jig. Cut the front rail out of the quarter inch plywood, cut the back rail out of the scrap wood, and cut the guide boards out of the quarter inch plywood as well. Use the following setup for the straight socket jig:

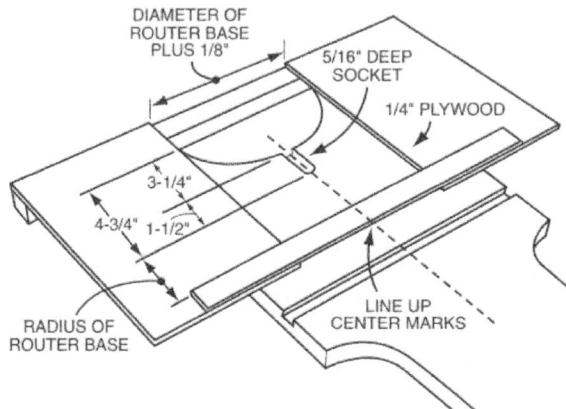

Set the straight socket jig to the centerline of the back. Line up both centerlines then clamp both the back part and the jig to the workbench. Set your router on the opening and then make 5/16" deep cuts to make the socket. Do the same steps to make the socket on the front (marked as part C).

The through dovetail will require a bit more of your manual carpentry skills since it is usually made by hand. Make sure to create precise cuts with the dovetail saw. You will also do a lot of chiseling to make the pieces fit. However, you can also use a router with the dovetail jig to make these precise joints rather quickly.

Assemble the without gluing any parts yet. Make sure that both the front and the back parts are square with the seat. Set the stretcher on the assembly so that you can mark the actual distance of the dove tail sockets. Cut the stretcher accordingly.

On the router table, shape the stretcher's dove tail ends. Make sure to test the fence using a scrap piece.

Assemble the front of the stool and glue them together. Turn it upside down and then drop the stretcher in. Allow the glue to dry. Plane the sides when the glue has dried so that the pieces are flush.

Now its time to make the two side rails. Cut them to the proper length and glue them. Make sure to clamp them in place. Sand the entire seat after the glue dries.

CHAPTER 7

TIPS ON STAINING AND FINISHING

It is easy to get tempted to cut your sanding work short. Sometimes you will also be tempted to get the preparation part done faster. Note that you should avoid doing both since these phases of woodworking are important when you're trying to produce high quality finish.

FINISHING AND STAINING REMINDERS

✓ Allow all stains and finishes to dry thoroughly

✓ Always test finishes and stains on scrap wood first

✓ Make sure to wipe the rim of every can so that the lid won't get sealed tight.

✓ Always clean brushes when they are used for oil based finishes

✓ Always ease all the edges

✓ Sand all surfaces before applying stain

✓ Use mineral spirits on damp cloth to wipe down on your pieces

✓ When using maple, porous hard wood, or softwood, coat the surface with wood conditioner before applying a stain or finish.

✓ Allow 5 to 15 minutes for the wood to absorb the wood conditioner. Wipe the excess away. This will ensure an even finish later on.

Printed in Great Britain
by Amazon

35398193R00046